DREAM JOBS IN
GREEN AND SUSTAINABLE LIVING

CYNTHIA O'BRIEN

CRABTREE
PUBLISHING COMPANY
WWW.CRABTREEBOOKS.COM

CUTTING-EDGE CAREERS IN TECHNICAL EDUCATION

Author:
Cynthia O'Brien

Series research and development:
Reagan Miller

Editorial director:
Kathy Middleton

Editor:
Petrice Custance

Proofreader:
Lorna Notsch

Design, photo research, and prepress:
Katherine Berti

Print and production coordinator:
Katherine Berti

Photographs:
Fotolia
Ingo Bartussek: p. 12
iStockphoto
FlairImages: p. 8 (bottom)
Jaakko Heikkilä: p. 9 (bottom left, house and solar panels)
mediaphotos: p. 24 (top)
Shutterstock
Filipe Frazao: p. 27 (bottom)
Fotos593: p. 6 (bottom right)
Martchan: p. 25 (bottom left)
Scott Prokop: p. 21 (bottom left)
Vadim Orlov: p. 10 (bottom left)
Wikimedia
Old Dane: p. 11 (bottom)
Stepheng3: p. 17 (center left)
All other images by Shutterstock

Library and Archives Canada Cataloguing in Publication

O'Brien, Cynthia (Cynthia J.), author
Dream jobs in green & sustainable living / Cynthia O'Brien.
(Cutting-edge careers in technical education)
Includes index.
Issued in print and electronic formats.
ISBN 978-0-7787-4440-5 (hardcover).--
ISBN 978-0-7787-4451-1 (softcover).--
ISBN 978-1-4271-2031-1 (HTML)
1. Environmental sciences--Vocational guidance--Juvenile literature.
2. Environmentalism--Juvenile literature. 3. Industries--Environmental aspects--Juvenile literature. I. Title.
GE60.O27 2018   j333.72023   C2018-900261-1
C2018-900262-X

Library of Congress Cataloging-in-Publication Data

Available at the Library of Congress

Crabtree Publishing Company
www.crabtreebooks.com   1-800-387-7650

Printed in the U.S.A./052018/CG20180309

Published in Canada
Crabtree Publishing
616 Welland Ave.
St. Catharines, Ontario
L2M 5V6

Published in the United States
Crabtree Publishing
PMB 59051
350 Fifth Avenue, 59th Floor
New York, New York 10118

Published in the United Kingdom
Crabtree Publishing
Maritime House
Basin Road North, Hove
BN41 1WR

Published in Australia
Crabtree Publishing
3 Charles Street
Coburg North
VIC 3058

CONTENTS

JOBS WITH SKILL

Do you like fixing or building things? How about creating cool hairstyles or planting gardens? If you answered yes, then Career and Technical Education programs will prepare you for your dream career. The jobs of the future are waiting for you!

WHAT IS CAREER AND TECHNICAL EDUCATION?

Career and Technical Education (CTE) programs combine academic studies, such as math and science, with valuable hands-on training. CTE students develop job-specific skills that are in high demand by employers.

CTE programs are divided into 16 career clusters. Some examples of these clusters are Information Technology (IT), Education and Training, Manufacturing, Hospitality and Tourism, and Marketing. Each CTE career cluster is divided into job pathways. Each job pathway is a grouping of jobs that require similar interests and paths of study.

DID YOU KNOW?

Ganado High School, located on the Navajo Reservation in Ganado, Arizona, offers an exciting range of CTE programs. Courses include nursing, architectural **drafting**, culinary arts, and even veterinary science!

In an age of growing **cybersecurity** threats, IT managers have a very important job. They maintain a company's **network** security and prevent unauthorized users from accessing company data.

EXPLORING YOUR OPTIONS

There are so many career paths to take, why not have fun finding out about them? Online quizzes can help match your interests with possible CTE careers. If you want some real-life experience, there are fairs and competitions you can attend, such as the SkillsUSA and Skills Canada championships.

Check out the CTE introductory programs that are offered in your area. Most high schools and some middle schools have them. There are also CTE summer camps where you can work on cars, master some cooking skills, or explore computer activities. It's exciting to think about your future, and it's great to start planning. Just remember that you don't have to choose one career path right now.

Food growers often sell their fresh produce at local farmers' markets.

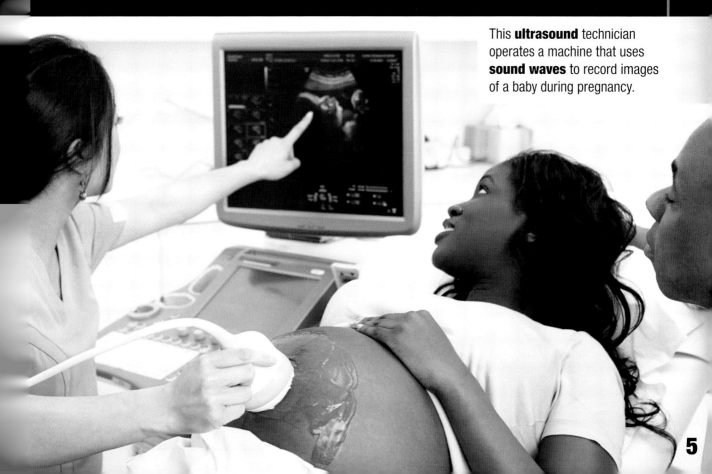

This **ultrasound** technician operates a machine that uses **sound waves** to record images of a baby during pregnancy.

THE FUTURE IS GREEN

Choose a green career and help protect Earth

Taking care of our planet has never been more important. Earth's resources are in danger from **deforestation**, pollution, and climate change. By working in a green and **sustainable** living career, you can help fight these problems. Green living means keeping our natural resources safe and cutting down on waste and pollution. Many CTE career clusters have pathways to green jobs, and many high schools include a green element in their CTE courses. Think about what interests you. If you like construction, you might consider becoming a green roof installer. Do you want to improve the way we grow our food? You could become a sustainable agriculture technician. The prospects are bright for young people looking to make a difference.

DID YOU KNOW?

In 2016, there were nearly 10 million green jobs worldwide. By 2030, that number is expected to reach 24 million.

Every day, 400 million pounds (181 million kilograms) of waste are dumped into water systems around the world.

Organizations in **renewable** energy, such as WRISE (Women in Renewable Industries and Sustainable Energy) in the United States and WIRE (Women in Renewable Energy) in Canada, provide support for women entering or already in the industry.

HOW TO USE THIS BOOK

Each two-page spread focuses on a specific career in Green and Sustainable Living. For each career, you will find a detailed description of life on the job, advice on the best educational path to take (see right), and tips on what you can do right now to begin preparing for your dream career. Let's get started!

GREEN AND SUSTAINABLE LIVING JOB PATHWAYS:

YOUR PATH

SECONDARY SCHOOL

This section lists the best subjects to take in high school.

POST-SECONDARY

Some jobs require an **apprenticeship** and **certification** while others require a college or university degree. This section gives you an idea of the best path to take after high school.

AGRICULTURE, FOOD, AND NATURAL RESOURCES	Green jobs in this pathway include sustainable agriculture technician and biomass farmer.
ARCHITECTURE AND CONSTRUCTION	Green roof installers and green building technicians help to make structures energy efficient.
INFORMATION TECHNOLOGY	Computer systems administrators may work on energy-efficient technology to help businesses waste less electricity.
MANUFACTURING	Green workers make solar panels and wind **turbines**.
SCIENCE, TECHNOLOGY, ENGINEERING, AND MATHEMATICS	Green and sustainable jobs in this pathway might include dealing with dangerous waste.
TRANSPORTATION, DISTRIBUTION, AND LOGISTICS	Green jobs include working on electric cars and reducing pollution from other transport vehicles.

SOLAR PANEL
INSTALLER

...ping to harness the Sun's power

Imagine living without electricity. Every day, you use it for so many things, from turning on a light to powering up your computer. Solar panel installers help to keep the power on with **photovoltaic** (PV) panels. These glass panels contain **solar cells** that soak up the Sun's energy and turn it into electricity. This solar energy heats buildings, water, and swimming pools. Solar energy is a fast-growing field, and solar panel installers are in high demand. The U.S. Bureau of Labor Statistics estimates the number of jobs will rise by 105 percent by 2026. That means opportunity for you!

ON THE JOB

Most of the time, solar panel installers work as part of a team. They spend much of their day outside, and sometimes work high up. Many installers work on homes and other buildings, but there is also work building large solar farms. The work involves measuring the site and building whatever supports the panels need. If you want to be a solar panel installer, you should like working with your hands. Using power tools, installers attach the panels and connect them safely to the electrical system. Afterward, installers test the panels and do maintenance checks.

DID YOU KNOW?

Elon Musk, the head of Tesla, has a vision of the United States one day being powered entirely by solar energy. He believes 100 miles (160 km) by 100 miles (160 km) of solar panels is all that is needed to supply power for the whole country.

Across the United States, about 5,500 schools are solar powered. Students at these schools enjoy close-up learning about clean energy.

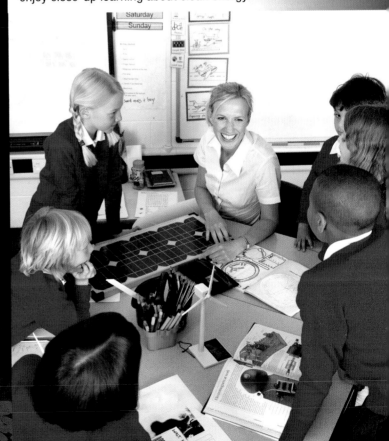

MEET A SOLAR PANEL INSTALLER

Wyatt Atkinson is a solar installation supervisor for GRID Alternatives in northern California. Originally from Montana, Wyatt spent four years in the U.S. Navy before studying Industrial Technology at Montana State University. While interning in Washington, Wyatt was certified by the North American Board of Certified Energy Practitioners (NABCEP) and worked on his first solar installations. After graduating, Wyatt, a member of the Assiniboine and Sioux tribes of the Fort Peck Reservation, became a part of GRID's tribal program. Wyatt loves his job because he can work with people and with his hands. He is passionate about teaching new volunteers and spreading the knowledge about clean, renewable energy. His goal is to bring solar energy to his tribe in Montana. This would give the tribe independent ownership of this amazing, sustainable energy resource.

DID YOU KNOW?

By 2025, all federal government buildings in Canada will be completely powered by renewable energy sources, such as solar power.

Solar-powered **microgrids** are bringing electricity to many rural African communities for the first time. Residents can now run lights and refrigerators, and they no longer need to walk to larger towns to access electricity to charge their cell phones.

YOUR PATH TO WORK AS A SOLAR PANEL INSTALLER

SECONDARY SCHOOL

Courses in electronics, technology, and science are useful.

POST-SECONDARY

Some companies offer apprenticeship programs. College graduates can earn certification from NABCEP.

You can't be afraid of heights in this job! These solar panel installers are securing solar panels into place on a rooftop.

WHAT CAN YOU DO NOW?

Research how solar power works. Search online for safe-for-kids solar power experiments that you can try. You could even arrange a solar energy cook-off at your school! EnergyWhiz is an annual competition that takes place at the Florida Solar Energy Center. Students design and build solar cookers. Then they demonstrate how well the solar cookers work by preparing original dishes for the judges.

WIND TURBINE
TECHNICIAN

A clean energy career that helps capture the power of the wind.

Become a part of the amazing developments in wind energy! By the end of 2016, there were more than 340,000 wind turbines around the world. There are more turbines installed every year. These powerful machines capture wind energy and turn it into electricity. Wind turbine technicians install, maintain, and repair the 8,000 parts that make up a single turbine. To do the job well, these "windtechs" have mechanical and electrical skills. They also understand wind science and other aspects of **meteorology**.

ON THE JOB

Wind turbines can be installed on land or at sea. Many are over 220 feet (70 m) high—almost as tall as the Statue of Liberty! Turbine technicians must be comfortable working up high where they clean, repair, or replace parts. They must be physically fit, as well, to cope with climbing the towers. Technicians must also be able to read and interpret plans and diagrams from engineers.

To keep safe, technicians wear harnesses and helmets when working high up on wind turbines.

WHAT CAN YOU DO NOW?

Learn everything you can about how wind power is harnessed. Search online for experiments with wind that you can try at home. See if there are any renewable energy clubs or competitions in your area that you can get involved with.

BZEE, a German organization, is a world leader in wind energy technology. More than 14,000 students from 12 countries have received BZEE certification, including students from Holland College in Prince Edward Island, Canada.

YOUR PATH TO WORK AS A WIND TURBINE TECHNICIAN

SECONDARY SCHOOL

Computer, physics, mechanical, and electrical courses provide good basic training for future wind turbine technicians.

POST-SECONDARY

Colleges provide wind turbine technician certificate programs. Many colleges offer BZEE certification.

DID YOU KNOW?

In February 2018, the communications company AT&T announced that it would be switiching a large portion of its power use to wind energy. This reduction in pollution will be the same as taking more than 350,000 cars off the road!

The powerful winds that blow over oceans are perfect for harnessing energy. The Anholt offshore wind farm in the Kattegat Sea, off the coast of Denmark, is one of the largest in the world. Denmark produces more wind energy than any other country in the world. Wind power supplies 42 percent of the country's electricity.

ENERGY
ADVISER

Help find new and better ways to stop wasting energy.

THERMAL CAMERA

We need advice about many things. For example, your school guidance counsellor can advise you about courses you can take. Today, many people want to make their homes or other buildings energy efficient, but they don't know how. They need an energy adviser, or **auditor**, to help them. These professional **consultants** inspect buildings and offer energy-saving solutions. They are also energy **advocates** who help to educate people about energy efficiency.

Blower door tests are used by energy advisers to check for air leaks in homes. A fan sucks air out of the home. Air will then flow into the home only through leakage points. An adviser goes from room to room to find leaks so they can be sealed.

ON THE JOB

Government departments, universities, energy companies, and other organizations employ energy advisers. Advisers spend time writing up reports and analyzing test results, but this is not just an office job. At other times, they are on-site at the buildings they are inspecting. They spend time talking to building owners or managers and to other energy professionals. After being called to a building, an adviser runs different tests to see where energy might be wasted. For example, an adviser can check for gas leaks with a mixture of dish soap and water that is sprayed onto gas hoses and pipes. If there is a leak, bubbles will form. After completing their tests, energy advisers recommend to an owner how best to make a building more energy-efficient, along with an estimate of the costs that will be involved.

DID YOU KNOW?

The United States uses about 24 percent of the world's energy but has only 5 percent of the world's population.

WHAT CAN YOU DO NOW?

Learn about the various forms of energy and how they are produced. Research energy use and energy **conservation**. Try doing an energy audit of your own home or school. Can you spot areas where energy could be used more efficiently?

There is much you can do to help cut down on energy use around your own home. Turn taps off while brushing your teeth, turn lights off when you leave a room, and close curtains on hot days to block the Sun's heat. You can even ask an adult to help you plant a tree to add cooling shade outside your home.

YOUR PATH TO WORK AS AN ENERGY ADVISER

SECONDARY SCHOOL

Courses in math, science, and computers help prepare you for energy advising work.

POST-SECONDARY

Colleges offer training in energy auditing. Many energy advisers have university degrees, such as environmental engineering.

DID YOU KNOW?

Energize Schools is a program in California that runs an annual energy conservation competition for schools. The school with the highest reduction in electricity use wins $900.

A career-training program developed by Stacks+Joules is teaching Boston-area high school students how to manage computerized power systems in modern buildings, with an emphasis on energy conservation. Most buildings do not run efficiently for energy savings, and there is a shortage of skilled workers to run the complex systems.

SUSTAINABLE AGRICULTURE
TECHNICIAN

A natural approach helps keep the land healthy.

Imagine a career in which you can help protect the food we eat. Sustainable agriculture technicians do just that. Sustainable agriculture is all about producing food using methods that are good for the land, animals, and people. For example, sustainable farmers do not use harmful **pesticides** on their crops. They use natural methods, such as introducing helpful insects to eat the pests. They also keep the soil fertile by rotating their crops and using natural **fertilizers**. Sustainable agriculture technicians work with farmers and researchers to help develop more eco-friendly ways to manage crops and animals.

You can buy an entire farm in a box! Freight Farms is a Boston-based company that sells recycled shipping containers as fully functioning sustainable farms. A variety of leafy greens and vegetables can be grown inside the containers with **hydroponics**, which can use up to 90 percent less water than traditional farming.

ON THE JOB

Agricultural technicians have the best of two worlds. They combine their love of the outdoors with their science smarts in the lab. They take soil and plant samples from the field and analyze them in the lab. Technicians often work for colleges, universities, or government agencies such as the Department of Agriculture. They keep records over time, so they can keep track of changes to plants, soil, and temperature. Technicians may also use their experience to start and manage their own farms.

DID YOU KNOW?

By 2050, the world's population is expected to reach 9 billion people. Agricultural production will need to increase in a sustainable way in order to meet this increased food need while also protecting the environment.

MEET A SUSTAINABLE AGRICULTURE TECHNICIAN

When she was younger, Laura Kemp wanted to be a doctor. But, after spending some time working on vegetable farms, she became interested in agriculture. So, she got a degree in **agronomy**, studying plant science and crop production. Today, Laura works for The Land Institute in Kansas, a sustainable agriculture research organization. Though she started there as an agricultural technician, she's now a field station manager. Laura still spends a lot of time in the field, doing everything from plowing and tending crops to changing the oil in the tractor. She also gathers samples to analyze in the lab. Every day is different, and there are always problems to solve—both things that Laura loves about her job. She's also passionate about using her science training to make a positive difference in the way we grow our food. One day, she might take all her knowledge and experience and start her own farm!

WHAT CAN YOU DO NOW?

Volunteer at a farm or start your own garden. Learn all you can about growing plants, including soil conditions and sustainable farming methods. Join a young farmers' association.

Farming First is an organization dedicated to promoting sustainable agricultural practices around the world, as well as improving the well-being of agricultural workers, especially women. In **rural** India, approximately 75 percent of women work in agriculture.

YOUR PATH TO WORK AS A SUSTAINABLE AGRICULTURE TECHNICIAN

SECONDARY SCHOOL

Biology and chemistry courses are excellent preparation for agricultural careers.

POST-SECONDARY

In college, a sustainable agriculture program includes training on a farm, lab work, and business courses.

Researchers believe **microbes** are the key to helping farmers increase their food production in a sustainable way. Microbes in the soil can help a plant better absorb nutrients, as well as provide protection against drought, disease, and pests—all without harmful pesticides and fertilizers.

DID YOU KNOW?

Agriculture employs 40 percent of the global population, making it the largest source of employment in the world.

GEOTHERMAL
DRILLING TECHNICIAN

Making use of Earth's natural energy

Powerful and rich clean energy resources lie from 10 feet (3 m) to many miles beneath Earth's surface. Hot springs and volcanoes are evidence of the heat stored inside Earth. Resource drilling technicians who specialize in **geothermal** drilling help to tap into this renewable energy source. They use special **rigs** that drill under the surface to reach hot liquids. The steam released from underground turns a turbine and creates electricity. For homes, technicians install underground pipes. Cool water runs down the pipes, absorbs Earth's heat, and returns hot water to the house.

ON THE JOB

Drilling technicians should like working outside, since this is where they spend much of their time. They work as part of a drill crew that includes people cleaning the drill site and engineers. The first job is to find the best location for a geothermal well by drilling test wells. Then they use heavy equipment and fluid to break up the rock to start drilling. Some technicians work on large-scale projects, while others work on geothermal heating for homes and businesses.

Iceland is a pioneer in the use of geothermal energy. Twenty-five percent of the country's total electricity production comes from geothermal power.

DID YOU KNOW?

Iceland has between 30 and 40 active volcanoes and many more that are inactive. It also has many hot springs. The country takes advantage of these resources, and geothermal energy heats 90 percent of homes. Workers with the Iceland Deep Drilling Project have created one of the world's deepest geothermal wells. It is almost 3 miles (4.5 km) deep, and the temperature at that depth is 800°F (427°C).

The Geysers in California is the world's largest geothermal field. It consists of 22 geothermal plants and more than 350 wells.

This worker is preparing to drill a geothermal well for a residential geothermal heat pump.

YOUR PATH TO WORK AS A RESOURCE DRILLING TECHNICIAN

SECONDARY SCHOOL

Geography, science, and mechanics classes provide a useful background for a drilling career.

POST-SECONDARY

Many colleges offer programs specializing in renewable energy and drilling.

This diagram shows geothermal heat pumps at work. Cold water is pumped down, heated inside Earth, then resurfaces as hot water.

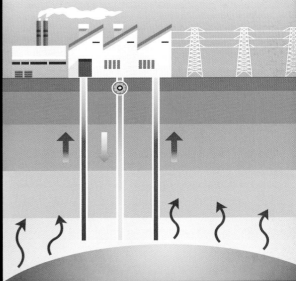

WHAT CAN YOU DO NOW?

Learn all you can about geothermal energy. Research different kinds of drilling rigs to learn how they operate. See if there is a renewable energy club in your area that you can join— or start your own!

BIOMASS
FARMER

Help grow energy

Corn tastes great, but it has another important use. It can be turned into a **biofuel** called **ethanol**. Other plants, such as wheat, sugarcane, and soy, are also sources of **biomass** energy. This energy comes from living **organisms**. Biomass farmers grow energy-giving crops and collect manure. Some farmers grow crops, such as canola and sunflowers, and use some for food and the rest for biofuel. Only biomass can be made into liquid fuels such as ethanol and biodiesel. The bioenergy industry needs more farmers to invest in this kind of production. If you want to be a farmer, you could be growing energy for the future!

WHAT IS BIOPOWER?

Energy companies change biomass into heat and electricity, or biopower, in one of three ways. Burning biomass produces steam to drive a turbine and create electricity. As the biomass rots, it produces a gas that can be used for electricity. Finally, some biomass is converted into a bio-oil that can be used for fuel.

ON THE JOB

All farmers have busy days throughout the year. Before planting seeds, farmers prepare their fields by tilling them with a tractor and plow. This can take weeks on a large farm. As the crops start to grow, farmers tend them by removing weeds and fertilizing the plants. At harvest time, farmers collect their plants to sell. Biomass farmers may use some of the plants to fuel their farm machinery, such as tractors. They sell the rest to energy companies.

Corn

Canola

Sugarcane

WHAT CAN YOU DO NOW?

Join a young farmers' group. Learn all you can about biomass farming and how the crops are converted into bioenergy. Research what plants will grow best in your area, depending on weather and soil conditions, and try planting your own garden.

The United States is the largest producer of corn in the world. Roughly 90 percent of the ethanol produced in the U.S. comes from corn.

YOUR PATH TO WORK AS A BIOMASS FARMER

SECONDARY SCHOOL

Science classes and CTE courses in agriculture, mechanics, and business are an important start.

POST-SECONDARY

Colleges and universities offer plant science programs, and farming associations provide training, internships, and apprenticeships.

Using biofuel in cars creates less pollution, which is better for the environment.

Wheat

Soybeans

Sunflowers

ENVIRONMENTAL
MANAGEMENT TECHNICIAN

Protecting and restoring the land

Do you love the outdoors and want to protect it? Environmental management technicians help to do this. They are problem solvers who look for sustainable ways to use natural resources and keep our **ecosystems** safe from harm. This means helping to stop pollution and other damage. Technicians may specialize. A forestry technician, for example, keeps track of a forest's growth. He or she watches over an area to protect against deforestation.

DID YOU KNOW?

The Sustainability Treehouse in West Virginia was built for the Boy Scouts of America. It is a completely self-sufficient building that produces its own power through solar panels and wind turbines. The building's water comes from collected rainwater that is cleaned in an on-site water-cleansing system.

Caring For Our **Watersheds** is an environmental contest for students that began in Canada and has since spread to the United States and Argentina. Students must research a local watershed, pinpoint an environmental concern in the watershed, and propose a real-world solution.

When an ecosystem is damaged, environmental management technicians work to **restore** it. First they remove the source of the damage, such as human access, sources of pollution, or damaging weeds. Then they work to restore health to the ecosystem by reintroducing plant and animal species that had disappeared from the ecosystem or by planting new types of vegetation.

ON THE JOB

Sustainable agricultural technicians work for the government, private companies, and conservation organizations. In the field, technicians take note of the numbers and types of wildlife and plants and collect soil and water samples. They use tools such as a geographic information system (GIS) to help them plot information on a map. In the lab, technicians study the samples and other information they have collected. They look for such things as **contaminants** and growth patterns and write reports on their findings. These test results help to make restoration and protection plans for the future.

WHAT CAN YOU DO NOW?

Join an environmental awareness club or start one at your school. Learn all you can about some of your local ecosystems and the threats they face. Plant a garden and research how to keep it healthy. Be aware of how your own actions affect the environment every day.

This GIS system allows technicians to record and monitor information about the health of specific ecosystems.

YOUR PATH TO WORK AS AN ENVIRONMENTAL MANAGEMENT TECHNICIAN

SECONDARY SCHOOL

Biology, chemistry, math, and computer courses all help with a future technician job.

POST-SECONDARY

Environmental technology college programs include training in ecosystem management and soil and water quality.

DID YOU KNOW?

EarthTeam is an organization in California that empowers youth to take the lead in caring for the environment. The group offers internships to help prepare students for careers in environmental management.

With a downloadable app such as iNaturalist, you can contribute to environmental scientfic research! Share your nature observations with research groups and fellow nature lovers with just a click of your phone.

GREEN ROOF
INSTALLER

Create living roofs for greener cities.

Love working outside and watching things grow? You could become a green roof installer. A green roof is a roof made of plants that grow over layers of other materials. Green roofs have many benefits, from improving air quality to keeping buildings warm or cool. Green roofs are a growing trend across North America, as cities adopt green policies. Qualified installers are more in demand than ever. In 2016, there were almost 900 new projects across North America reported to Green Roofs for Healthy Cities (GRHC).

ON THE JOB

This green career combines construction skills with a knowledge of plants and landscaping. Installers work mostly outside and should be comfortable working up high. After installing the underlying roof structure, it is time for planting. It can take over a million plants to cover a large roof. These plants must be able to grow together and suit the climate. A green roof professional (GRP) knows how to make this happen and selects the right plants for the job.

Green roofs look beautiful, and they can save you money! The plants provide a building with insulation and shade, which help to lower energy costs.

New York City is located on the Atlantic Flyway—a **migration** route from the Arctic to South America for more than 200 different species of birds. The growing number of green roofs in the city is supplying these birds with valuable resting and feeding spots.

WHAT CAN YOU DO NOW?

Research green roofs and learn about the many environmental and cost benefits they offer. Study how green roofs are made and how they function, including the layers involved in their construction and the materials required. Try planting your own garden, learning as much as you can about which plants grow best in your area and why. Try adding features to attract birds or insects to your garden, such as a cut piece of orange to attract butterflies.

YOUR PATH TO WORK AS A GREEN ROOF INSTALLER

SECONDARY SCHOOL

Biology, science, and CTE classes in construction, landscaping, and agriculture are helpful.

POST-SECONDARY

Many colleges offer green roof courses, and GRHC provides professional certification.

In 2009, Toronto was the first city in North America to pass a bylaw that requires green roofs on new buildings over six stories high. According to a 2016 GRHC survey, Toronto had more green roofs than any other city in North America, followed by Chicago.

There is a farm in the heart of bustling downtown Toronto! Ryerson University's Andrew and Valerie Pringle Environmental Green Roof contains a rooftop farm that produces 10,000 pounds (4,536 kg) of produce every year.

GREEN
ARCHITECTURAL
TECHNICIAN

Help to design environmentally friendly buildings.

Do you want to combine your love of building design with your passion for the environment? Become a green architectural technician! These technicians work with engineers, contractors, and architects to draw up building guidelines. Green architecture technicians want to help make buildings sustainable. This includes installing renewable energy systems and using recyclable or **biodegradable** building materials where possible. With their specialist training in green building design and renewable energies, green architectural technicians are helping to build the future!

ON THE JOB

Architectural technicians are not architects, but they do work with design and construction plans. Usually, they use computer-aided design (CAD) programs to create plans that include information such as the measurements of materials and costs. They are good communicators who keep in touch with the architect and construction team and make changes to the plans as necessary. Architectural technicians work for architectural, construction, and engineering companies. They spend time in the office, but also make visits to the building site.

Rainwater tanks are a simple and effective way to help a home go green. Rainwater is captured and then used for watering gardens, flushing toilets, and laundry. This helps homeowners to reduce water use and save on water bills.

These green architectural technicians are installing triple-glazed windows. The three layers of glass better stop heat from escaping than traditional double-glazed windows.

WHAT IS LEED?

Leadership in Energy and Environmental Design® (LEED) is an internationally recognized rating system for green buildings. It is used in more than 160 countries for all kinds of buildings. The rating system awards points. For example, there are LEED points for buildings using renewable energy sources and for water protection, such as using **gray water**. Location is also very important. LEED awards points for building projects that protect or restore some of a site's natural surroundings.

WHAT CAN YOU DO NOW?

Research LEED and learn all you can about green building practices. Check online for CAD demonstrations or activities that you can try. Join an environmental awareness club or start one of your own. Set a goal for you and your family to reduce energy consumption in your home.

YOUR PATH TO WORK AS A GREEN ARCHITECTURAL TECHNICIAN

SECONDARY SCHOOL

Math, art, and computers as well as CTE courses in CAD and engineering design, if available, are an excellent start.

POST-SECONDARY

Many colleges offer architectural technician courses, including courses on green building. LEED exams lead to LEED Green Associate or specialist credentials.

DID YOU KNOW?

The U.S. Green Building Council and Canada Green Building Council offer training for green architectural technicians.

Bosco Verticale is a pair of residential towers in Milan, Italy. The towers were awarded LEED Gold, the highest level of energy certification. The towers include 730 trees, 5,000 shrubs, and thousands more smaller plants. The vegetation helps to reduce pollution, produce oxygen, reduce noise, and control temperatures in the buildings, reducing energy costs.

For a building to receive LEED certification, its systems must have high energy-efficiency ratings. Energy-efficient thermostats better control a building's temperature, reducing energy waste and cost. Some thermostats can even regulate temperatures within different rooms of a building.

HYDROPOWER
TECHNICIAN

Working with water-powered energy

Using water power for energy is not a new idea. As early as 300 B.C.E., rushing water was used to turn wheels to grind wheat into flour. Today, the hydropower industry uses dams to capture water for electricity. Large dams, such as the Grand Coulee Dam, on the Columbia River in Washington, produce enough power to supply more than 2 million homes every year. Water is a renewable resource. However, dams can have damaging effects on surrounding ecosystems. Scientists are looking at new water power sources, such as ocean **tides** and waves.

ON THE JOB

At a hydropower plant, a technician inspects and maintains machinery, such as turbines and pumps. Repairs and new installations of equipment are a regular part of the work. Technicians also inspect tunnels and make sure that water is flowing freely. They monitor, or keep track of, the energy that the turbines produce. As the hydropower industry explores new technologies, there is plenty of exciting opportunities for green-thinking technicians.

This giant tidal turbine will be powered by tidal force to create electricity. Much research is going into this renewable source of energy as tides are more predictable than the Sun and wind.

The Bay of Fundy in Nova Scotia has the world's highest tides. More than 176 billion tons (160 billion metric tons) of water move in and out of the bay every day, twice a day! Scientists and engineers are working to use these powerful waves to create electricity.

WHAT CAN YOU DO NOW?

If there is a hydropower plant or dam in your area, see if you can arrange a tour. Learn all you can about how water is harnessed for energy, both in hydropower plants and from ocean waves. Research the different kinds of dams and how they function, as well as their effect on local ecosystems. Join a local renewable energy club or start your own.

Inside a hydroelectric power plant, huge turbines are turned by rushing water to create electricity.

YOUR PATH TO WORK AS A HYDROPOWER TECHNICIAN

SECONDARY SCHOOL

Science, math, and CTE classes in electricity and machine technology are great beginnings.

POST-SECONDARY

Many companies provide on-the-job training, and some offer apprenticeships. College certificates in renewable energy and electricity are also a good idea.

DID YOU KNOW?

A new wave-energy testing site is due to open in Newport, Oregon in 2020. The site will test wave-energy converters, which harness the energy of ocean waves and turn it into electricity.

A technician sits in the control room of a dam, monitoring its computerized systems.

WATER AND WASTEWATER LABORATORY TECHNICIAN

The world needs clean, safe water. As a water and wastewater lab technician, you would be a water quality champion.

If you like to work in a lab and solve problems, a career as a water and wastewater laboratory technician could be for you. These technicians can work in many different places, including treatment plants, consultancy companies, and the government. Technicians study water to prevent disease and harm to the environment. They monitor the processes involved in the collection and treatment of water. They also look for treatment solutions for **industrial waste**.

ON THE JOB

Field work, such as collecting water samples, is part of a technician's job. Water technicians take samples from water treatment plants, lakes, sewers, pools, and wells. They might also visit a testing site to look for evidence of pollution. Some testing can be done in the field, but most of the time, technicians work in the lab, studying samples, or in an office writing reports. Testing and reports need to be done before and after water is treated.

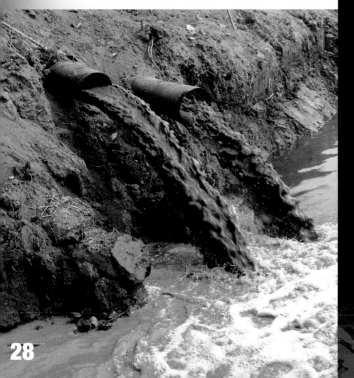

Every year, 1.2 trillion gallons (4.5 trillion liters) of untreated **sewage** and industrial waste are dumped into U.S. waters.

The water that comes out of your tap comes from a water treatment plant. Here, the water goes though a number of cleaning and testing processes before it is safe for you to use.

WHAT CAN YOU DO NOW?

Ask your teacher to arrange a tour for your class of your local water treatment plant. Research the steps required for safe, clean water to reach your tap. Join a water conservation or environmental awareness club, or you could even start your own. Learn about the different kinds of pollutants that threaten our waters and the steps being taken to protect the water.

This technician is collecting a wastewater sample. The sample will be taken to a lab and tested for levels of contamination.

YOUR PATH TO WORK AS A WATER AND WASTEWATER TECHNICIAN

SECONDARY SCHOOL

Chemistry and biology courses and CTE classes in environmental technology are excellent places to start.

POST-SECONDARY

A college degree in water and wastewater is usually required, and certification in wastewater management or water conservation is available.

DID YOU KNOW?

Earth Rangers is a Canadian conservation organization for kids. More than 175,000 members learn about the importance of sustainable living through hands-on conservation projects.

In the lab, technicians test and analyze the safety levels of water samples. Testing is done before, during, and after treatment.

LEARNING
MORE

BOOKS

Brezina, Corona. *Jobs in Sustainable Energy.* Rosen, 2010.

Dakers, Diane. *Green Ways of Getting Around: Careers in Transportation.* Crabtree, 2011.

Gazlay. Suzy. *Re-Greening the Environment: Careers in Clean-Up, Remediation, and Restoration.* Crabtree, 2011.

Johanson, Paula. *Jobs in Sustainable Agriculture.* Rosen, 2010.

Owen, Ruth. *Building Green Places: Careers in Planning, Designing, and Building.* Crabtree, 2009.

Owen, Ruth. *Growing and Eating Green: Careers in Farming, Producing, and Marketing Food.* Crabtree, 2009.

Roza, Greg. *Internship and Volunteer Opportunities for People Who Love Nature.* Rosen, 2013.

WEBSITES

WWW.ONETONLINE.ORG	A career search site that provides education and skills requirements
HTTPS://CLIMATEKIDS.NASA.GOV/ MENU/DREAM	NASA site about green careers
HTTPS://GRIDALTERNATIVES.ORG/WHAT WE-DO/WORKFORCE-DEVELOPMENT/ SOLARCORPS-FELLOWSHIPS	Solar installation training at GRID Alternatives SolarCorps Fellowship program
WWW.EPA.GOV/CAREERS/ STUDENT-INTERNSHIPS	Intern with the Environmental Protection Agency (EPA)

GLOSSARY

advocate Someone who supports a cause

agronomy The science of crop and soil management

apprenticeship A period of time spent learning skilled work with hands-on training

auditor Someone who examines a situation and reports their findings

biodegradable Able to break down without harm to the environment

biofuel A fuel produced from biological raw materials

biomass Energy source from living or recently living plant materials or animal waste

certification Certificate that shows someone has achieved a certain level of skill and knowledge

conservation Protection of animals, plants, and natural resources

consultant Someone who gives professional advice

contaminant Something that pollutes

cybersecurity Protecting a computer system from unauthorized access

deforestation Cutting down or burning all trees in an area

drafting The drawing of sketches or plans

ecosystem Everything that exists in a particular place, including living things such as animals and plants, and non-living things such as rocks.

ethanol A type of alcohol that can be used as a clean-burning fuel source

fertilizer A substance, such as manure, that is added to soil to help plants grow

geothermal The natural heat energy from Earth

gray water Household wastewater that does not contain serious contaminants

hydroponics The growing of plants in nutrient solutions instead of soil

industrial waste Materials left over from factories, mines, and other industries

meteorology Science dealing with weather and atmosphere

microbes Microscopic germs

microgrid A small-scale power grid

migration The movement from one region to another

network A system of computers connected through communication lines

organism A living thing

pesticide Chemical used to destroy insects or animals that harm crops

photovoltaic Converting sunlight into electricity

renewable Able to be replaced naturally

restore Return something to its original condition

rig A piece of equipment designed for a specific purpose

rural In the country, as opposed to a city or town

sewage The waste contents of a sewer or drain

solar cell A device that converts sunlight into electricity

sound waves Energy waves that carry sound

sustainable Able to be used without destroying or using up

tide The daily rise and fall of Earth's oceans

turbine An engine with blades turned by water, steam, or air pressure

ultrasound The use of sound waves and other vibrations to create a digital image

watershed An area of land that catches rain and snow and drains into a body of water

INDEX